First World War
and Army of Occupation
War Diary
France, Belgium and Germany

27 DIVISION
Divisional Troops
19 Brigade Royal Field Artillery
15 October 1914 - 29 April 1915

WO95/2257/4

The Naval & Military Press Ltd
www.nmarchive.com
Published in association with The National Archives

Published by

The Naval & Military Press Ltd

Unit 10 Ridgewood Industrial Park,

Uckfield, East Sussex,

TN22 5QE England

Tel: +44 (0) 1825 749494

www.naval-military-press.com

www.nmarchive.com

This diary has been reprinted in facsimile from the original. Any imperfections are inevitably reproduced and the quality may fall short of modern type and cartographic standards.

© **Crown Copyright**
Images reproduced by permission of The National Archives, London, England, 2015.

Contents

Document type	Place/Title	Date From	Date To
Heading	WO95/2257/4		
Heading	27th Division Divl Artillery 19th Brigade R F.A Dec 1914-Dec 1915		
Heading	27th Division 19th Bde. R.F.A. Vol I 19.12.14-31.1.15		
War Diary	Winchester	19/12/1914	19/12/1914
War Diary	Havre	20/12/1914	22/12/1914
War Diary	St Omer	22/12/1914	22/12/1914
War Diary	J Piuescure	23/12/1914	02/01/1915
War Diary	Renescure	03/01/1915	07/01/1915
War Diary	Pradelles	08/01/1915	09/01/1915
War Diary	Heksken	13/01/1915	16/01/1915
War Diary	Dickebusche	17/01/1915	31/01/1915
Miscellaneous	A Form Messages And Signals.		
Heading	27th Division 19th Bde. R.F.A. Vol II 1-28.2.15		
War Diary	Dickebusche	01/02/1915	28/02/1915
Miscellaneous	A Form. Messages And Signals.		
Miscellaneous	5th Corps Summary Of Information No 10	07/03/1915	07/03/1915
War Diary	Dickebusche	01/03/1915	25/03/1915
Heading	27th Division 19th Bde. R.F.A. Vol IV 1-30.4.15		
War Diary	Dickebusch	31/03/1915	03/04/1915
War Diary	Watou	04/04/1915	07/04/1915
War Diary	Westhoek	08/04/1915	30/04/1915
Heading	27th Division 19th Bde R.F.A. Vol V 1-31.5.15		
War Diary		01/05/1915	31/05/1915
Miscellaneous	The Officer Commanding		
Heading	27th Division 19th Bde. R.F.A. Vol VI 1-30.6.15		
War Diary		01/06/1915	30/06/1915
Miscellaneous	Nominal Roll Of Officers		
Heading	27th Division 19th Bde R.F.A. Vol VII 1 18-4-15		
War Diary		01/07/1915	18/07/1915
Heading	27th Division 19th Bde R.F.A. Vol VIII Sept 15		
War Diary	19th Bde R F A Head Qre	01/09/1915	01/09/1915
War Diary	39th Battery		
War Diary	95 Battery		
War Diary	96th Battery		
War Diary	131st Battery		
War Diary	19th Bde A Column		
War Diary		17/09/1915	27/09/1915
Map			
Miscellaneous	Translations		
Heading	27th Division 19th Bde. R.F.A. Vol IX Oct 15		
War Diary	19 Bde Hqrs	01/10/1915	01/10/1915
War Diary	39th Battery R F A	01/10/1915	01/10/1915
War Diary	95th Battery R F A	01/10/1915	01/10/1915
War Diary	96th Battery R F A	01/10/1915	01/10/1915
War Diary	131st Battery R F A	01/10/1915	01/10/1915
War Diary	19th Bde. A. Column	01/10/1915	01/10/1915
War Diary	19th Bn R F A	07/10/1915	24/10/1915
Heading	27th Div 19th Bde R.F.A. Nov Vol X		
War Diary	19th Bde H. Qrs	15/11/1915	15/11/1915

War Diary	39th Bty R.F.A.	15/11/1915	15/11/1915
War Diary	95th Bty R.F.A.	15/11/1915	15/11/1915
War Diary	96th Bty R.F.A.	15/11/1915	15/11/1915
War Diary	131st Bty R.F.A.	15/11/1915	15/11/1915
War Diary	19th Brigade A. Column	15/11/1915	15/11/1915
War Diary		13/11/1915	13/11/1915
Heading	27th 19th Bde R.F.A. Dec Vol XI		
War Diary	19th Bde R.F.A. H.Qu	01/12/1915	01/12/1915
War Diary	39th Bty R F A	01/12/1915	01/12/1915
War Diary	95th Bty R.F.A.	01/12/1915	01/12/1915
War Diary	96th Bty R.F.A.	01/12/1915	01/12/1915
War Diary	131st Bty R F A	01/12/1915	01/12/1915
War Diary	19th Bde A. C.	01/12/1915	01/12/1915
War Diary	19th Bde S. A. A. Section	01/12/1915	01/12/1915
War Diary		03/12/1915	16/12/1915
Heading	27th Division 95th Batty R.F.A. Vol I 15.10.14-31.1.15		
War Diary	India	15/10/1914	31/01/1915
Heading	27th Division 95th Batty 19th Bde R F A Vol II 1-27.2.15		
War Diary	Dickebusch	01/02/1915	27/02/1915
Heading	27th Division 95th Batty. R.F.A. Vol III 1-31.3.15		
War Diary	Dickiebusch	01/03/1915	31/03/1915
Heading	27th Division 131th Batty R F A Vol I 27.11.14-31.1.15		
War Diary	Winchester	27/11/1914	19/12/1914
War Diary	Havre	21/12/1914	21/12/1914
War Diary	Renescure	07/01/1915	07/01/1915
War Diary	Pradelles	08/01/1915	08/01/1915
War Diary	Heksken	17/01/1915	17/01/1915
War Diary	Dickebusch (H.35. Q.5.0)	17/01/1915	25/01/1915
War Diary	Dickebusch (H.28d.3.1)	26/01/1915	31/01/1915
Heading	27th Division 131st Batty (19th Bde) RFA. Vol II 31.1-27.2.15		
War Diary	Dickebusch (H28d 3.1)	31/01/1915	13/02/1915
War Diary	Samepos	14/02/1915	27/02/1915
Heading	27th Division 131st Battery (19th Brigade) RFA. Vol III 28.2-29.3.15		
War Diary	Samepos	28/02/1915	29/03/1915
Heading	27th Division 131st Batty R.F.A. Vol IV 31.3-29.4.15		
War Diary	Westhoek	09/04/1915	29/04/1915

Woods /225 4/4

27TH DIVISION
DIVL ARTILLERY

19TH BRIGADE R.F.A.
DEC 1914-DEC 1915

27TH DIVISION
DIVL ARTILLERY

27th Division

19th Bde. R.F.A.

121/4264.

Vol I. 19.12.14 — 31.1.15.

Head Quarters
19th Bde R.F.A.

Sheet 1.

Army Form C. 2118.

WAR DIARY
or
INTELLIGENCE SUMMARY
(Erase heading not required.)

Hour, Date, Place	Summary of Events and Information	Remarks and references to Appendices

Winchester 19/12/1914	19th Brigade Royal Field Artillery 27th Div Artillery
	
	Lt Col: W Maclean R.F.A. Commanding
	Lt G Temple R.F.A. Adjutant
	
	95th Battery R.F.A. { Major Broadrick F.B. A(SR)
	     Comdg 27° { 2Lt MacDonald J(SR)
	            { 2Lt Hinworth G(SR)
	            { 2Lt Alchin H
	
	96th " Major Smythe G { 2Lt Sulzeur F(SR)
	          Comdg: { 2Lt Carberry
	                   { 2Lt Simpson R(SR)
	
	131st " Capt Maubey J { 2Lt Hinwood H(SR)
	          Comdg: { 2Lt Timm C(SR)
	                   { Lt Geldeen R(SR)
	
	A Col: Capt Plomley W { Lt Dolvee C(RofO)
	           Comdg: (T) { 2 Lt Robinson S(T)
	                    { Lt Cecil A(T)
	
	Attached { Capt Chambers G (RAMC)
	              Lieut Hunter T S (AVC)
	              Interprete M. Allen Mellt (Tem: Comm:)
	                                    (12th Cuirassiers)	

2nd Sheet

WAR DIARY
INTELLIGENCE SUMMARY.
(Erase heading not required.)

Army Form C. 2118.

Instructions regarding War Diaries and Intelligence Summaries are contained in F. S. Regs., Part II and the Staff Manual respectively. Title pages will be prepared in manuscript.

Hour, Date, Place	Summary of Events and Information	Remarks and references to Appendices
9 AM. 19-12-14 Winchester	The Bde proceeded by March Route from Winchester to Southampton, arrived at Southampton Docks at 7.30 PM. Embarked as follows:— Head Qr Staff — S.S. Norian 95th BRFA — S.S. City of Chester 96th " " — S.S. City of Benein 131st " " — S.S. Norian A Col. — S.S. City of Dunkirk	
Noon 20-12-14 Havre	Sailed at 11.30 PM. arrived at Havre. Remained on board until dusk, disembarked & stopped in Hangars at quay side for night.	
5 AM 21-12-14 Havre	Entrained at Point-I en route for St. OMER. drew five days supplies	
22-12-14	Remained in train. Travelled during night. Route via ROUEN, arrived at St. OMER 7.30 AM.	
7.30 AM 22-12-14 St. OMER	Detained at St. OMER. Proceeded to RENESCURE by march route via ARQUE. arrived noon. Hd. Qrs. billeted at CHATEAU-de-PALMART.	

Army Form C. 2118.

WAR DIARY
or
INTELLIGENCE SUMMARY.

3rd Sheet

(Erase heading not required.)

Instructions regarding War Diaries and Intelligence Summaries are contained in F. S. Regs., Part II. and the Staff Manual respectively. Title pages will be prepared in manuscript.

Hour, Date, Place	Summary of Events and Information	Remarks and references to Appendices
23-12-14 Renescure to 2-1-15	Training, Instruction to Telephonists & squadron inspection by Col Comdg, Clothing Equipt. Rations etc. Three horses died, three horses transferred to A.V.C. Mobile Section, 1 one horse (J.T.D) joined from ST OMER.	
9 AM 3-1-15 Renescure	Brigade inspected by Brid Genl Stokes, Comdg 27th Div Arty, at junction roads, RENESCURE-EBBLINGHAM, ¼ mile W. of LYNDE.	
9 AM 4-1-15 Renescure	Received orders to be ready to move early. Bar. inspected by Col. Comdg.	
5-1-15 Renescure	Received orders to move on 7-1-15 at 8 AM	
6-1-15 Renescure	Training	

WAR DIARY
INTELLIGENCE SUMMARY.

(Erase heading not required.)

Army Form C. 2118.

4th Sheet

Hour, Date, Place	Summary of Events and Information	Remarks and references to Appendices
8 AM 7-1-15 Renescure	Bde proceeded by March Route to PRADELLE via EBBLINGHEM, WALLON CHAPELLE, HAZEBROUCK Railway crossing & BORRE.	[sig]
8-1-15 Pradelles	Ordered to stand fast, be ready to move H.Q. at 8 AM on 9th inst. One gunner of Bde Staff admitted to H.P. Three men of A Col wounded by rifle accident	[sig]
9 AM 9-1-15 Pradelles	Brigade left PRADELLES enroute for HEKSKEN via BAILLEUL and WESTOUTRE arrived at billets at 3 PM.	[sig]
10th to 13th -1-15 Heksken	Training, + rest.	[sig]
14-1-15 Heksken	Training, + rest. Signaller injured from misuse of Revr by rifle, reported to APM (suspected espionage)	[sig]
15-1-15 Heksken	Brigade receives orders to be in readiness to proceed to firing line on 17-1-15.	[sig]
2 AM. 16-1-15 Heksken	Brigade moved to firing line in recently of DICKEBUSCHE in relief of 20th Bde RFA.	[sig]

WAR DIARY or INTELLIGENCE SUMMARY.

Army Form C. 2118.

5th Sheet.

Hour, Date, Place	Summary of Events and Information	Remarks and references to Appendices
17-1-15 Dickebusch	Special instructions issued to OC 95, 96 + 131 Batteries regarding preparations for night firing, also to OC AC. The Order was given by Army of saving lines + horseflesh. Copy of Telephone message to BM attached. Progress:-	Order to OC AC:- xxx Unless otherwise ordered the Bde AC will daily take enough transport to IJAC to draw 20 rds per gun. xxx [signed]
18-1-15 Dickebusch	Reserve ration checked + reported to Adj. On as 16 regiments ten horses received from Mobile section AVC, + posted as follows:- Head Quarters - 2 Riding 95th Batty RFA - 2 - do - - 6 Draught	[signed]
19-1-15 Dickebusch	Instructions issued regarding "progress reports", "Any occurrence of importance is to be telephoned at once	[signed]
20-1-15 Dickebusch	Capt. G.H. Merriman arrived from RHA to take over command of ACI.	[signed]
21-1-15 Dickebusch		

WAR DIARY
INTELLIGENCE SUMMARY

1st Sheet
Army Form C. 2118.

(Erase heading not required.)

Instructions regarding War Diaries and Intelligence Summaries are contained in F.S. Regs., Part II and the Staff Manual respectively. Title pages will be prepared in manuscript.

Hour, Date, Place	Summary of Events and Information	Remarks and references to Appendices
22-1-15 Dickebusch		
23-1-15 Dickebusch	2nd Lt Feilden ACol transferred to Home Estabt.	BT
24-1-15 Dickebusch		BT
25-1-15 Dickebusch	No 31901 Gnr William Maxim died suddenly of heart failure. (A.Col)	BT
26-1-15 Dickebusch	Orders issued that the Bde less 457 Bty would return to Billets at HERSKIN. Order cancelled. Stand fast.	
27-1-15 Dickebusch	Bde strengthened by 67th Bty & the 20th Bde RFA.	BT
28-1-15 Dickebusch	Telephone line laid from Bde Hd Qrs to VOORMEZEELE	BT
29-1-15 Dickebusch	Telephone wire from Bde Hd Qrs at Restaurant to SHELL infantry trenches. No. 4 B Section	BT
30-1-15 Dickebusch		BT
31-1-15 Dickebusch		[signature]

"A" Form.
Army Form C. 2121.

MESSAGES AND SIGNALS

Prefix	Code	m.	Words	Charge	This message is on a/c of:	Recd. at	m.
Office of Origin and Service Instructions			Sent At 6.44 PM m. To RA By Cpl Mahon (Signature of "Franking Officer.")		Service.	Date 17-1-15 From By	FA1

TO	Bde Arty	Maj	27th	Div
*	Sender's Number	Day of Month	In reply to Number	AAA

Daily progress report AAA HQ
AAA 95th By opened
fire at 9.49 AM on enemy trenches
situated on square A7B sheet 26 SW
1/20000 after our trenches had been
shelled by the enemy 8 rounds were
fired and seemed to be well
distributed over the target. Range a
little long differing for each gun
AAA 96th By draining trenches and
making cover AAA 131 By 6 PM
17-1-15 improving our epaulments +
digging bomb proofs

From: O6 19th Bde RFA
Place:
Time: 6-40 PM

The above may be forwarded as now corrected.
(Z) JJ G Temple
Censor. Signature of Addressor or person authorised to telegraph in his name
*This line should be erased if not required.

7th Division.

19th Bde: R. + A.

Vol II 1 - 28.2.15

WAR DIARY or **INTELLIGENCE SUMMARY.**

Army Form C. 2118.

Head Quarters
19th Bde RFA
7th Street

Hour, Date, Place	Summary of Events and Information	Remarks and references to Appendices
1-2-15 Tickebush	2nd Lt St Ann 95th Battery RFA is posted Lt 19th Bde A Col.; Captain Merriman takes over comd of 95th RFA & 131st Battery Spend time + line Sd-Ste LOI	95th RFA vice Major Brodrick
9.55 PM		
2-2-15 Tickebush	Lt Carhery transferred to RHA rode Bde fund	
3-2-15 Tickebush	Lt Carhery transferred to RHA from RFA.	
4-2-15 Tickebush	Lt Timm Ingrasiene to RHA for instruction, replaced by St Murray RHA. The Brigade shoed Just Dames up + stood packed ready to move. Orders received at 8.45 P.M.	

Army Form C. 2118.

Hd Qrs
19th TDd RFA
8th Sheet

WAR DIARY
or
INTELLIGENCE SUMMARY.
(Erase heading not required.)

Instructions regarding War Diaries and Intelligence Summaries are contained in F.S. Regs., Part II. and the Staff Manual respectively. Title pages will be prepared in manuscript.

Hour, Date, Place	Summary of Events and Information	Remarks and references to Appendices
5/2/15 Buckenwald		[sig]
6/2/15 Buckenwald		[sig]
7/2/15 Buckenwald	3 Drivers arrived from base joined HQ & 95th TD RFA. Major Broadrick rejoined from sick leave and assumed cmd 95th TD Bty R.F.A.	[sig]
8/2/15 Buckenwald		[sig]
9/2/15 Buckenwald	Capt. Merriman to ACol vice Capt. Plenty reported sick. Lt 395. Batty RFA joined the Brigade as 2nd Lt.	[sig]

Army Form C. 2118.

WAR DIARY
or
INTELLIGENCE SUMMARY.
(Erase heading not required.)

Instructions regarding War Diaries and Intelligence Summaries are contained in F.S. Regs., Part II and the Staff Manual respectively. Title pages will be prepared in manuscript.

Hour, Date, Place	Summary of Events and Information	Remarks and references to Appendices
10/2/15 Tjikeurach	Capt. Flenley procedure on sick leave	[sig]
11/2/15 Tjikeurach		[sig]
12/2/15 Tjikeurach		[sig]
13/2/15 Tjikeurach		[sig]
14/2/15 Tjikeurach	At 4 PM Message received from HQ - S.O.S. The Brigade stood to + continued in action during the night.	[sig]
15/2/15 Tjikeurach	Action still in progress. Wire received at 7.45 AM telephone Message from HQ. Telephonic communication. From HQ attached	Telephone Message attached

WAR DIARY
or
INTELLIGENCE SUMMARY.

Army Form C. 2118.

Hour, Date, Place	Summary of Events and Information	Remarks and references to Appendices
16.2.15 Fjeldwich		
17.2.15 Fjeldwich		
18.2.15 Fjeldwich		
19.2.15 Fjeldwich		
20.2.15 Fjeldwich		

117

Army Form C. 2118.

H.Q. Sect.
15 R.E. 11
Sgd 11/7

WAR DIARY
or
INTELLIGENCE SUMMARY.
(Erase heading not required.)

Instructions regarding War Diaries and Intelligence Summaries are contained in F.S. Regs., Part II and the Staff Manual respectively. Title pages will be prepared in manuscript.

Hour, Date, Place	Summary of Events and Information	Remarks and references to Appendices
21-2-15 Richebourg	One horse died (sent) one horse HS received from 11 A.T. battery. One driver joined brigade & posted 39/B/5. Two Staff Sgt. Fuller (War personel) joined brigade from England & posted at Busiet. 1695+96 Boiting Capt. Rollo RE (Sig Co) attached returns to his unit.	[sig]
22-2-15 Richebourg		[sig]
23-2-15 Richebourg		[sig]
24-2-15 Richebourg		[sig]
25-2-15 Richebourg		[sig]

Army Form C. 2118.

WAR DIARY
or
INTELLIGENCE SUMMARY.

(Erase heading not required.)

HQ "B" RFA
1915 / Sept 1-2

Instructions regarding War Diaries and Intelligence Summaries are contained in F. S. Regs., Part II and the Staff Manual respectively. Title pages will be prepared in manuscript.

Hour, Date, Place	Summary of Events and Information	Remarks and references to Appendices
26.2.15 Tickelnah	Draft arrived from Base & posted as follows:— 39 F. 13 R. — 1 Bomb. 1 Sgt Filler. 96 " 1 Cnpl. 1 Gunner. 13 " 1 Bomb. 1 Gunner. 1 F.M. 1 Shoeing smith. A.C 1 Bomb. 2 Serjts. 1 Bomb.	[signature]
Tickelnah 27.2.15		[signature]
Tickelnah 28.2.15		[signature]

"A" Form.
Army Form C. 2121.

MESSAGES AND SIGNALS.

No. of Message 136

Prefix	Code GA m.	Words 37	Charge	This message is on a/c of:	Recd. at 7.30 A m.
Office of Origin and Service Instructions.		Sent			Date 15.2.15
RA	At 7.45 A m.		Service.	From RA
	To All Bty			By Lt Temple
	By Cpl Ma[kenzie]	(Signature of "Franking Officer.")	

| TO | 19th BDE | | |

Sender's Number	Day of Month	In reply to Number	AAA
BM 508	15th		

following Received from 82nd Infy Brigade at 7.0 AM begin. all Trenches now Reoccupied AAA very Grateful to RA for Tremendous help ends Please communicate to all Ranks

From	BM
Place	
Time	7.35 AM

The above may be forwarded as now corrected. (Z)

Censor. Signature of Addressor or person authorised to telegraph in his name
*This line should be erased if not required.

118 A

"A" Form.　　Army Form C. 2121.

MESSAGES AND SIGNALS.　　No. of Message _____

Prefix **SM**　Code **HZA**　Words **39**　Charge _____

Office of Origin and Service Instructions: **RA**

Sent At _____ m. To _____ By _____

This message is on a/c of : _____ Service.

(Signature of "Franking Officer.")

Recd. at _____ m.　Date _____　From _____　By _____

TO: **19 BDE**

Sender's Number	Day of Month	In reply to Number	AAA
BM 509	15		

following received by 27TH DIVISION for General Plumer 5TH corps begins Well done AAA congratulations to General LONGLEY and his troops and to General STOKES and his Guns ends

From **BM**

Place _____

Time **5.45 AM**

118 B

"A" Form.

MESSAGES AND SIGNALS.

Prefix	Code	Words	Charge	This message is on a/c of:	Recd. at
	C*pt*				
				Service	Date
					From
				(Signature of "Franking Officer.")	By 67

TO — **G O C R A**

Sender's Number	Day of Month	In reply to Number	AAA
GR/56	2		

Your artillery as usual contributed invaluable assistance to infantry last night AAA GOC wishes to express his thanks to you and through you to OC Batteries and Brigades concerned

From: 27 Div
Place:
Time: 8 40 AM

The above may be forwarded as now corrected. (Z)

Censor. Signature of Addressor or person authorised to telegraph in his name

*This line should be erased if not required.

Extract

5th Corps
Summary of Information No 10
7-3-15

ALLIES' FRONT
x x x x

The German trenches in front of ST. ELOI were bombarded & the bt. installed with considerable amount of success.

Some reprisals were probably during the day & good execution has been made on the enemy's main trenches in that neighbourhood.

It is reported that the German troops in the trenches suffered severely.

x x x x

(sd) V Spence ?
for Brig: Gen: G.S. 5th Corps

659.

WAR DIARY
or
INTELLIGENCE SUMMARY.

(Erase heading not required.)

Army Form C. 2118.

HQ 19th Bde 1?

Hour, Date, Place	Summary of Events and Information	Remarks and references to Appendices
Dickebusch 1-3-15	Brigade	657
2-3-15	Brigade engaged in ReLining Trenches & Supports of Infantry attack Corps Orders from G.O.C. attached. Attack commenced 12.30 AM and firing ceased firing at 3 a.m.	
3-3-15		
4-3-15		
5-3-15		

WAR DIARY
INTELLIGENCE SUMMARY
(Erase heading not required.)

Army Form C. 2118.

ALG 1915
Summary

Hour, Date, Place	Summary of Events and Information	Remarks and references to Appendices
6/3/15	Shell & enemy trenches. Commenced 6.30 AM, 8hlt 12 Noon. 3.15 PM — 5.50 PM	Intelligence Summary 4 reports attached
7/3/15	Pte R. Ross died.	
8/3/15	Draft arrived from base. Total as follows: Sgts — 2, Cpls — 6, L/Cpls — 5, Ptes — 4, ACs — 3	
9/3/15		
10/3/15		

ND GHQBEF

WAR DIARY
INTELLIGENCE SUMMARY
(Erase heading not required)

Army Form C. 2118.

67

Hour, Date, Place	Summary of Events and Information	Remarks and references to Appendices
11.3.15		
12.3.15	Bn Recce received from Col Mold Relief BOESCHEPE to a place one died at 7-3-15	
13.3.15		
14.3.15	Opened fire on German Trenches at ST ELOI at 5 PM to assist our infantry in repulsing heavy German attack	
15.3.15	Several trenches int by our Troops also "Mound" Counter attack opened at 2AM. some trenches reoccupied	

Army Form C. 2118.

664

WAR DIARY
or
INTELLIGENCE SUMMARY.

(Erase heading not required.)

H.Q. 2ndM.R. 19th Sheet

Hour, Date, Place	Summary of Events and Information	Remarks and references to Appendices
16.3.15		
17.3.15		
18.3.15	G. Harper adults to P. (N.Y.II)	
9.3.15		
20.3.15		

Instructions regarding War Diaries and Intelligence Summaries are contained in F.S. Regs., Part II and the Staff Manual respectively. Title pages will be prepared in manuscript.

Army Form C. 2118.

WAR DIARY
or
INTELLIGENCE SUMMARY.
(Erase heading not required.)

666

Hour, Date, Place	Summary of Events and Information	Remarks and references to Appendices
21. 3. 15		
22. 3. 15		
23. 3. 15	391. Battery withdrawn from firing line & forwarded via Boischeste	
24. 3. 15		
25. 3. 15		

121/54/21

27th Division

19th Bde: R.I.H.

Vol IV. 1 — 30.4.15.

Army Form C. 2118.

WAR DIARY
or
INTELLIGENCE SUMMARY.
(Erase heading not required.)

Instructions regarding War Diaries and Intelligence Summaries are contained in F.S. Regs., Part II. and the Staff Manual respectively. Title pages will be prepared in manuscript.

Hour, Date, Place		Summary of Events and Information	Remarks and references to Appendices
Dickebusch	31.3.15	Capt. J.C. Hawley left the battery for no. 18 Anti-aircraft Section. Capt. G.H. Freeman took over temporary command. Battery did not fire.	From 19th Bde A.H.Q.
do.	1.4.15	Right Section was relieved by one section of 107th Bty at 9.45pm. Battery did not fire.	
do.	2.4.15	Left section relieved by another section 107th Bty at 9.45pm.	
do.	3.4.5	Battery marched into rest billets 1½ miles East of WATOU	
WATOU	4.4.15	Major C.R. Hill R.H.A. from no. 18 Anti-aircraft section assumed command of battery.	
"	5.4.15.	Battery remained in rest billets & were inspected by Genl. Plumer.	
"	6.4.15.	Right Section left WATOU at 8 p.m. & relieved the French Battery in action at WESTHOEK at 4.30 a.m. 7.4.15. J.I.C. 6.6.	
"	7.4.15.	Left section left WATOU at 9.45 p.m. & relieved the French at WESTHOEK at 3 a.m. 8.4.15. J.I.C.6.6.	
WESTHOEK	8.4.15.	Did not fire.	

129

19th Bde RFA
April 1915
Army Form C. 2118.

WAR DIARY
INTELLIGENCE SUMMARY
(Erase heading not required.)

Hour, Date, Place	Summary of Events and Information	Remarks and references to Appendices
April 1st 19/15	Brigade withdrew from DICKEBUSCH having been in action fully still in action and marched to new billets in WATOO	
April 2nd 19/15	Remaining resting the withdrawn units again shook and were relieved by 23rd Bde and afforenoon. Lt/Col Mackean & Major Brooke reconnoitred B.G.O. CRA WEST DIV and afternoon command of the Bde.	
April 3rd	Rest. Bde and Bty commanders reconnoitred positions they taken over from the French	
April 4th	Adj. F. went up to front positions	
April 5th	A section from each Bty 6th, 39th and bde Hy moved into front positions covering ground So of 7.64 (ON WOOD) Middle available Btys bivouaked when they could find room	
April 6th	Remaining sections of the two Btys moved up into action. First section of 9th and 131st came into action	

Army Form C. 2118.

WAR DIARY
or
INTELLIGENCE SUMMARY.
(Erase heading not required.)

Hour, Date, Place	Summary of Events and Information	Remarks and references to Appendices
April 7th	Remaining sections of 95 and 131 came into action.	
April 8th	Brigade zone from F.M.E. VERBEEK in J.10.a.0.5 to J.10.a.10.2. 39th and 96th Btys. from positions in J.7.a covered zone south of POLYGON WOOD. 131 and 95th Btys. in position J.5.a covered remainder of zone.	
April 9th 10 11 12 13 14 15 16 17 18 19 20	All quiet. Brigade covering front of 90th Brigade.	

WAR DIARY or INTELLIGENCE SUMMARY

Army Form C. 2118.

Hour, Date, Place	Summary of Events and Information	Remarks and references to Appendices
22nd April 19:15	In accordance with 85th & 134th Bde's [?] instructions 13th's next Bty in order to be ready to open fire towards St Julien (C12A)	
April 23rd	Obs. St opened up near farm C26c6↑. Which fire could be directed on Weltje – St Julien Rd. The Bttn had a very day on C10D3↑. The Battery [?] fire being not formed to C22 b 39. There returned all the Battery by (24th) in midst[?] track with G.O.C 3rd Canadian Inf Bde & directed the fire on targets as indicated by Div Staff	
April 24th		

19 WS A 1177A 123

Army Form C. 2118.

WAR DIARY
or
INTELLIGENCE SUMMARY.
(Erase heading not required.)

Instructions regarding War Diaries and Intelligence Summaries are contained in F.S. Regs., Part II. and the Staff Manual respectively. Title pages will be prepared in manuscript.

Hour, Date, Place	Summary of Events and Information	Remarks and references to Appendices

April 25th
Obs. St. about 400 yds W of FREZENBERG cross roads (D 25 c 2.8) where fire was directed on Wood in C 10 d & C 11 c, Thur on D8a, & on roads in D7. 8. Thur roads were Shelled except Honnybeck

April 26th
The night (25-26) Obs. Stn. moved to D 20 a 8.9 (H.Q. 37) Durng the day fire was directed with accuracy on enemy Support trenches & Pt on GRAVENSTAFEL Ridge. Fire continued at intervals through night

400,000. 9/14. H.&J.Ltd. Forms/C. 2118/10.

19th TRTA
124

WAR DIARY
or
INTELLIGENCE SUMMARY.
(Erase heading not required.)

Army Form C. 2118.

Hour, Date, Place	Summary of Events and Information	Remarks and references to Appendices
27th April	Vacancies to be formed in trenches as party of Reserve to the HAMBREEK valley, requested fired in afternoon. The staff as was again directed as roads in fire. I shortly returned and went to D9c2.6 it is returned to D9c2.6 at this time the Waggon lines hot E.16 YPRES were suffering very heavy from shell fire. A steady mvt as a 2nd A. coy fire maintained at night.	
28th April		

Army Form C. 2118.

WAR DIARY
or
INTELLIGENCE SUMMARY.
(Erase heading not required.)

Hour, Date, Place	Summary of Events and Information	Remarks and references to Appendices
29th April	As it was decided to bring fire further to E. the guns of 131st Bty had to be pushed out into the open line of fire about due NE. This gave the position away & Shell fire was sustained	
30th April	131 Guns had been run back but position was still shelled. Fired on D.9.19	

12/Sept

a2
a26

2nd Division

19th Bde R.F.A.
Vol IV 1—31.5.15.

Army Form C. 2118.

WAR DIARY
or
INTELLIGENCE SUMMARY.
(Erase heading not required.)

Hour, Date, Place	Summary of Events and Information	Remarks and references to Appendices
May 1st 1915.	Lieut Col L.M. Smyth was appointed to command 19th FA Bde. On the nightly of "2" one section forward Battery one battalion to position's 1.15 & 7.94 in front of him too 1.0 of bre evening. 95th Battery 1.9 & 4.3. South of Gunner Farm 700yds E of YPRES. 131 Battery on right of 95th Battery. 39th on right of 131 now Battery. The 161 & 75th Howitzer Batteries firing on the N entrance of GRAVENSTAFEL & road to YPRES. Major R.J.B.D. Bostock went sick. The Adjutant was killed by heavy howitzer fire N.E. of S.	
May 2nd	Lieut Sugarman J. Drewett & J. Ritchie being heavy attacks at the Angres of a Salient forward. But at big land at 2.50 am about Farm Cemetery and took care of lost the Germany	
May 3		

WAR DIARY
or
INTELLIGENCE SUMMARY.
(Erase heading not required.)

Army Form C. 2118.

Hour, Date, Place	Summary of Events and Information	Remarks and references to Appendices
May 4th	Lectures of the Brigade were Withdrawn, teller moving at 8.30 to for the lecture tent Book before the returned with Capts and without a Rest. The 19th H Q was established in the third buildin Ecole at BIENFAISANCE. Reuet 39th Battery was ordered to move in the St Munson Artillery and the 19th B/n was in the open & they attained to 1. N. e. 6.5. firing on South of Rue Sous The R/n gus were from U 13 & 5.1.6. 1.30 Z 23	
May 5th	96th Battey was ordered to position U.15 b 2.0. Atphine Lt Drummond cath - the powder and half an german further	
May 6	2 Lieut Recke 39th Battey wounded	

179

Army Form C. 2118.

WAR DIARY
or
INTELLIGENCE SUMMARY.
(Erase heading not required.)

Instructions regarding War Diaries and Intelligence Summaries are contained in F.S. Regs., Part II. and the Staff Manual respectively. Title pages will be prepared in manuscript.

Hour, Date, Place	Summary of Events and Information	Remarks and references to Appendices
May 8th	Enemy broke thro' the 28th Div. dn the right of the 27th Division but had to fall back. — The 39th Battery never being to get into action had from them — Orders received that owing to the way the Battery fought the Gunner of the German Attack was seriously shaken. They were firing most of the day smaller 18 pdr. losses even though they were firing about at the commencement of the day they going thru so much NE, & found at 16th n at German in the open, down at conclusion the infantry who retired at repose.) great confusion, the infantry who retired at repose.) After this the fire was silently. — The Hussars organised a mounted in convoys approachable our fire as soon during a considerable part of the day this was no hostile effort. I knew the Battery and the Gunners.	Casualties 6-5-15 22 S/Sgt. Copeland R — W 25 Bndr. Ratcliff J — W Dvr. Kerris J — W 26 Officers I J. Brown — W Sgt A — W P. Tett A — W R. Holt W — W J. Scopelon W 2-5-15 79 NK 80 NK 92 NK 131 NK Col. NK Casualties 8-5-15 29 Sgt. S/Sgt Grogie L Bndr. Parker J J 50 (T) Freshwater P.J. 93 NK Holland A B. Goulston A G. Hamon L 9 Lindell R

Army Form C. 2118.

WAR DIARY
or
INTELLIGENCE SUMMARY.
(Erase heading not required.)

Instructions regarding War Diaries and Intelligence Summaries are contained in F.S. Regs., Part II. and the Staff Manual respectively. Title pages will be prepared in manuscript.

Hour, Date, Place	Summary of Events and Information	Remarks and references to Appendices
May 8th/1st	Until time of attack was the 39th Div. in billets.	Casualties (not 7.9.17) 131. M.L. 95. M.L.
May 9th	Major [?] & Ruess, Lieut [?] Gibson & [?] Pultney, [?] Gasket Lieut. [?] Plu. was wounded.	Casualties 7.9.15 33. M.L. 93. G Campbell G 93. G Easter M 95. M. Gasket M Brig. Pluer M.L. 131. M.L. 95. nil
	The 39th Div occupied the front from trench 103 to YPRES. It began half to but the trenches began to run a front of 5000 yards. The trenches are like sniper shooting; no trolly trenches at all. attack in the South the enemy a trolly The[?] take in a stand further back so is not at all aware of the enemies.	Casualties 10-5-15 39 G Baxter JT W G Beal R.E. W Lieut SS Wyatt [?] W 1st Scots W 59. Fisher ? Mounsey M ? 9th Middlesex J M 9. Fowler J W 9. Allen G W 9. Salter G W 9. Cockrane T? W 9. Deelly H W 9. Christopher D W 9. Cluxton R W

131

Army Form C. 2118.

WAR DIARY
or
INTELLIGENCE SUMMARY.
(Erase heading not required.)

Hour, Date, Place	Summary of Events and Information	Remarks and references to Appendices
May 16	Officers with Brigade	Casualties
	Lieut Col E.A Smyth — Commanding	96 Nil
	Lieut G Tempe Adjt	131 P Burns R M
		Connaught TT-S-T
	Capt G.O'Hanlon M.O. Crowns Craig Office	39 Nil
	— R.A.M.C. Lieut A.S. Hinds A.V.C. Br Kuded	75 Nil
		96 G R Crooks G W
	39 Battery Major H.B Fitz Gerald	G Crooks G W
	2 Lieut B Gray	Sgt Tapp V W
	2 Lieut J Crist (attached from R Column)	Lt D Jones FT Injd
	2 Lieut E Dugan (on R Column)	a W
	75 Battery Major Manning Cox	
	Lieut A. McDonald	Maj 130 ingred
	2 Lt J.E. Hincott	L Lt Jones Tappe
	2 Lt G Aclum	Lieut Bryan 8/9/15
	96	
	2 Lieut E G Williams	
	2 Lieut DHM Cooley	
	2 Lt G McKew	

Instructions regarding War Diaries and Intelligence Summaries are contained in F. S. Regs., Part II. and the Staff Manual respectively. Title pages will be prepared in manuscript.

WAR DIARY
or
INTELLIGENCE SUMMARY.
(Erase heading not required.)

Army Form C. 2118.

Hour, Date, Place	Summary of Events and Information	Remarks and references to Appendices
May 10th	131 Batt Maj C H Holt 2 Lieut C E Tenne 2 Lieut J T Allen 2 Lieut A P Cole	All the Battery's guns got knocked out, & when they got two there was given one to 96th & one to 39th Maj Holt [illegible] comd of 9[illegible] [illegible] Maj [illegible] place
	Amm Coln Capt F A F. Morgan Capt A H Plumbly Lieut J A G Cecil (att'd to 39th). 2 Lieut J W Patterson Lieut A Ruddy	Joined brigade 8/5/15
	39th withdrew to position W of Canal to [illegible] G H Q line Battle continued all night – ~~[illegible]~~ [illegible]	
May 11	Battle continued ~~39th [illegible]~~	

Army Form C. 2118.

WAR DIARY
or
INTELLIGENCE SUMMARY.
(Erase heading not required.)

Hour, Date, Place	Summary of Events and Information	Remarks and references to Appendices
May 13.	Demonstration continues week - no change — Capt Morrison-Bell & 11th Sav'd officer — Lieut Temple R.E. on holiday — Captn Morgan R.G.A. relieved Lieut Potts in the city (Battlemora barracks 1.15720) The 95th Battery were withdrawn that night and the guns sent on 96 Batty — Maj. Argo's O.C. 96th reported that at a night map. [illegible] positions and the 13th [illegible] came through but not active. H battery was shelled up arm dolar area. 5.9 etc. 4·2 etc enemy had cover by no means B off'd the posts — To little showed in stability about 13.14 1st Batt'ns. 8 others fell in on the offices of 96th Battery wounding 2nd Lieut Buckley first intact Captain Morgan (15/249) Artillery officer Capt Temple [illegible] 96th Battery Capt Powell [illegible] 96 Batty	Casualties 12.5.15
		39 M.G.
		95 Sgt. Park J.S. F.M.
		W.
		B. Hubert A
		Dawson C
		Ross J.M.
		Lieut Swann C
		lieut Turpin R.E.
		96 Cpl Tow M.H.
		M
		All SS Perkins E
		S.M. Burrows W
		13.15 S.M. Pemberton J
		Gr Brown W
		M.G.
		A.C.
		[illegible names]
May 14.		

WAR DIARY
or
INTELLIGENCE SUMMARY.
(Erase heading not required.)

Army Form C. 2118.

Hour, Date, Place	Summary of Events and Information	Remarks and references to Appendices
May 15:—	Capt. & Parson, P.E. Jones ceased duty owing to S.M. R. m. W.	Crawley 13 Ord
	add. 96 "Batt. formation 2 Lieut Millar & Jones 24th evacuated	Gr. Isham T Dodd W a/c of staff T W
May 20 # 2 Lieut Escombe		Crowe J W
		Crowe W 14
May 16	14-5-15- 39 — Sergt. King G W.— W	
	G. Jennings W.— W	
	95 — nil	
	96 2Lt Carberry D Hn. W	
	2Lt Hulgar 2G W	
	131 nil	
	Col: Capt. Morgan Jas (R.G.A.) W.	
15-5-15	NIL	20-5-15- 131. G. Wadley R W
16.5.15	131. G.2 Losey W Drvr killed	21.5.15- 2nd Col. A.P. W
		Nil
17.5.15	G. Oleary T W	22.5-15- Nil
18-5-15	Lr Corp. George H.A.R. Munro	23.5.15-
	nil	
	Bq. Staff Mulley R W	
	131 G. Legon A W	
19.5.15	131 Cpl Gold H W	
	A.C.	

Gen. Sr. H. Plumer Comm. 2nd II army deprecates attacks.

135

WAR DIARY
or
INTELLIGENCE SUMMARY.
(Erase heading not required.)

Army Form C. 2118.

May

Hour, Date, Place	Summary of Events and Information	Remarks and references to Appendices
24-5-15. 3.15 a.m.	Very heavy gun fire kind, + a strong smell of gas - the enemy our gun, and the artillery fires all day - and then fire alone kept the enemy back as our cavalry retired. Away the front was absolutely knocked out by the gun, continued fighting till 10 p.m. Fourteen very machine 1000 yards of front - not an inch. troops every it, the entirely again kept the Germans out.	Casualties 24-5- Russell F. C^n Donnell Q. — W 131. O.C^n Rogers A W G. Johnson T W G. Lee A W G. Lahaie A K G. Croker C W Lt. Foster A K Lt. Hales T. W Lt. Hodson H W G. Judson J.H. W 39. Batt. 2.Lt Gray R. W B.S.M. Greensted, W. 9. Williams wounded base
25.6.	M.O. evening the 24 + 25 the declin caused by the fire of 19th B^n was not broken, the fire saved it. Nil	26. 5. 39th Batty. F^d Britten E.A. W.
26.	Nil	26. 39 P^t Mutchly E. Kich by him
27	Nil 2.Lt Tate E.O Jan 131	27. 3 Nil
28	2.Lt Tormey C.E Aamlin Infestal	
29.		

136
Y

May

Army Form C. 2118.

WAR DIARY
or
INTELLIGENCE SUMMARY.
(Erase heading not required.)

Hour, Date, Place	Summary of Events and Information	Remarks and references to Appendices
31-5-15	19th Bttn was relieved by 23rd Brigade. The 95th Batty and one section of each of the other Batteries marched to the MENEGATE near ARMENTIERES.	9th Feb. 30 A.F. Reply T W.

The

Officer Commanding,

        On the 22nd inst. General Sir H.Plumer, Commanding IInd Army, held a parade of the only two Batteries of the Division at rest, and addressed them as representing the whole of the Artillery of the Division, on behalf of the Commander-in-Chief, requesting the G.O.C.R.A. at the conclusion, to convey the gist of his remarks to all units of the R.A. under his Command, and these are therefore here recorded.

"   The Commander-in-Chief is as you know a "
" very busy man and is consequently not able to "
" visit all units, he therefore deputed me to see "
" you as representative of the Artillery of the "
" 27th Division, in order to convey to you his "
" personal thanks and deep appreciation of the "
" very excellent work done by Officers, N.C.O's "
" and men during the very arduous, trying and anx-"
" ious period of April 22nd to May 13th. Had it "
" not been for the determined resistance which was"
" shown on this front, not only might a further "
" withdrawal (even to the giving up of Ypres) have"
" been necessary, but it might have been incumbent"
" upon us to postpone the operations in the South."
"   The stand made round Ypres not only "
" allowed of these latter operations to be carried"
" out, but attributed in no small measure to their"
" success, further it no doubt influenced certain "
" other wavering Nations and States at a critical "
" moment. The Commander-in-Chief feels that "
" when the history of this great war is written, "
" the above will be found to be the case, and that"
" those who have fought in this severe second "
" battle of YPRES will, in days to come, be able "
" to look back with pride on their share in their "
" helping to affect the cause of the Allies. "
" During the winter fighting the Artillery did not"
" perhaps experience quite the hardships or casual"
" ties endured by the Infantry, but there can be "
" no doubt that during this battle they suffered "
" as heavily in the matter of casualties, and had "
" just as strenuous a time. "
"   Not only was great credit due for the "
" way the work was carried out at the gun posit- "
" ions, but also for the manner in which the "
" supply of ammunition was maintained without any "
" hitch whatever."

A. Stokes.

Brig-General.R.A.

23-5-15.   Commanding Royal Artillery, 27th Divn.

137

12/6034

24th Division

19th Bde: R.F.A.

Vol VI 1 — 30.6.16

27th Division

ar
a96

138

WAR DIARY
or
INTELLIGENCE SUMMARY.
(Erase heading not required.)

Army Form C. 2118.

Hour, Date, Place	Summary of Events and Information	Remarks and references to Appendices
June 1st	Remaining section of 19th Bgde moved to the Butts S of MENEGATE — and went into action about GRIS POT and BOIS GRENIER — The 39.95.131 Battery was under Lot NAP + Lt 96th Ballygaut Col. Dawson —	
June 6	moved 39.95.131 to N of ARMENTIERS + No 4 Warrant Howitzer Batty attacked — Zone covered from level crossing c 4 d. 9 to c 23 d 1.0.	
Jun 9	on night of 9th c 62 Batty attacked — on 11th c 6c howitzer attacked	

139

Army Form C. 2118.

WAR DIARY
or
INTELLIGENCE SUMMARY.
(Erase heading not required.)

Hour, Date, Place	Summary of Events and Information	Remarks and references to Appendices
On June 27th	82nd Inf: Bde moved slightly further South	
9.5am	Moved to position W of FLENQUE Fm on M4 28-29	
3pm	S of Cemety on 29-30	
30	Here bavec in lying	

[signature]

140

June 1915

WAR DIARY or INTELLIGENCE SUMMARY

Army Form C. 2118.

Hour, Date, Place	Summary of Events and Information	Remarks and references to Appendices
2 Jun	Nominal Roll of Officers.	2/Lt Miller att'd 39th Batt'y, returned to 111 Bde R.F.A.
	Head Quarters:- Lt. Col. G.A. Smyth, Lt. G. Smyth, Lt-Adjutant, MO, Capt L.O. Chambers M.D., Lieut L.P. Hands A.V.C.	2/Lt Escombe. R.F.C. returned to Eng'd
	39th Battery:- Maj M.J.F. Fitzgerald, Capt. E. Hodgkinson Smith, 2/Lt Corbett, 2/Lt. C.E. Bone.	aft. ten weeks att'd 96(Mely
	95th Battery:- Major L. Maber, Capt. C. Buzzer, 2/Lt. A. Alcohen, 2/Lt. G. Kenworth, 2/Lt Puddy	② Joined on 4th June
	96th Battery:- Capt. G.C. Neville, 2/Lt. G. H.C. Burton, 2/Lt H.B. Younge, 2/Lt. Faulkerton+Kennard ②	
	131st Battery:- Major- C.P. weds, 2/Lt. J.J. allen, 2/Lt B.C. Lister, Lt Turner.	Sick
	Amm. Col:- Capt W.H. Plomley, 2/Lt. E. Wilfred, 2/Lt. L. Lockwood, 1/Lt. A Ruddy, + a W² + 95th Batt'y	‖ Joined on 8/6/15
	Interptr. M. Muller	

37th Division

121/6401

19th Bde R.F.A.

1-8-4-15

Army Form C. 2118.

WAR DIARY
or
INTELLIGENCE SUMMARY.
(Erase heading not required.)

Instructions regarding War Diaries and Intelligence Summaries are contained in F.S. Regs., Part II. and the Staff Manual respectively. Title pages will be prepared in manuscript.

Hour, Date, Place	Summary of Events and Information	Remarks and references to Appendices
July 1st	**Nominal Roll of Officers**	
	Rank — Name	
19th Bde H.Q.	Lieut-Colonel — L.A. Smythe	absent in charge of hand
	Lieut — G. Temple	
attached	2/Lieut — W.M. Cedmore Medical Officer	
	Captain — L.O. Chambers A.V.C.	
	Lieut — F.B. Hunter	
39th Battery	Major — M.T.F. Fitzgerald	Transferred to 2015th Am. Col
	Captain — C. Hotchkinson Smyth	
	2/Lieut — C.E. Rose	
	Lieut — J. Cecil	att'd for on' est.
95th Battery	Major — K. Majors	
	Captain — C. Person	
	2/Lieut — A. Alchin	
	2/Lieut — G. Harworth	
96th Battery	Major — S.E. Neville	
	2/Lieut — G. McEwen	transferred to Base
	2/Lieut — H.S.B. Yorge	
131st Battery	Major — Zuckerton McKenan	
	2/Lieut — C.R. Nell	
	2/Lieut — L.T. Allen	
	2/Lieut — B.C. Lister	
	2/Lieut — A. Lowe Lt Tunnel	
Amm². Col.	Captain — M.H. Plomley	
	2/Lieut — L. Milford	
	2/Lieut — L. Lockwood	
	2/Lieut — A. Ruddy	every officer H.H.M.B.

143

Army Form C. 2118.

WAR DIARY
or
INTELLIGENCE SUMMARY.
(Erase heading not required.)

Instructions regarding War Diaries and Intelligence Summaries are contained in F. S. Regs., Part II. and the Staff Manual respectively. Title pages will be prepared in manuscript.

Hour, Date, Place	Summary of Events and Information	Remarks and references to Appendices
2.7.15. 131st Bty. B.A. Chunn	2/Lieut Torrie H.	Joined from Base. 30.6.15.
95th Bty.	2/Lieut George H.B.	Posted from 96th Bty. 2.7.15.
95th Bty.	Capt Penham G.E.	Rejoined 95th Battery 2.7.15
39th Bty.	Lieut Dabble G.	2nd Batt. W. Riding atts – 39th Bty. 28.7.15. for instruction
131st Bty.	2/Lieut McKay J.B.	Joined from Base 29.7.15
131st Bty.	2/Lieut Allen G.J.	Co. Stores. Establishment 29.7.15.
19th Bde N.R.	2/Lieut Ruddy	Co. Stores. Establishment 29.7.15.

Army Form C. 2118.

WAR DIARY
or
INTELLIGENCE SUMMARY.
(Erase heading not required.)

Hour, Date, Place	Summary of Events and Information	Remarks and references to Appendices
July. 18	62ⁿᵈ Inf" Bⁿ Relieves 19ᵗʰ Bⁿ from Front Tr LYS - PONT BALLOT with 679 Bally r 148 from A Group. 19ᵗʰ Bⁿ moves South. Lieut Irvine was post. A.D.C. item to 96ᵗʰ. Lieut Young " " " . thin invalided to considered line. A. General Booth.	

37th Division

19th Bde R.F.A.
Vol VIII
Sept. 15

121/6950

19th B'de R.F.A.

"O" B: RFA

WAR DIARY
or
INTELLIGENCE SUMMARY
(Erase heading not required.)

Army Form C. 2118.

Instructions regarding War Diaries and Intelligence Summaries are contained in F.S. Regs., Part II. and the Staff Manual respectively. Title pages will be prepared in manuscript.

Hour, Date, Place			Summary of Events and Information	Remarks and references to Appendices
Sept. 1. 1915			NOMINAL ROLL of OFFICERS	Joined Brigade
HQ 19 BDE RFA Head Qrs	RANK	NAME		
(attached)	Lieut Col.	E.A. Smyth		20.9.9
	Lieut	Semple		2.11.13
	2/Lieut	Thompson		14.11.14
	2/Lieut	Mulhead A.V.C.		2.7.15
	2/Lieut	Roberts R.A.M.C.		24.7.15
39th Battery	Major	Ant C. E. FitzGerald		10.29.15 { Major F. Hamilton, sub for 27 Dec
	Capt.	E.P. Ribblesdale		3.7.15
	Lieut	J. Cane		10.12.14 { 2/Lt 8.15
	2/Lieut	J. E. G. Burne		15.6.13 { 2/Lt Bowell 2/Lt Paden
95th Battery	Major	L.A.D. Nixon		29.5.15 F.A. Brigade
	Capt.	E. M. Wilcox		1.2.15 11 12 15
	Lieut	J. J. N. O'John		19.11.12 2/Lt L. Hilton
	2/Lieut	J.G. Balton		27.4.15 joined from dept 3 Jan 12.9.15
96th Battery	Major	2/c Neville		14.5.15
	2/Lieut	C. Whiteside		9.7.15
	2/Lieut	J.M. Timme		22.7.15
	2/Lieut	L.N.Y. O.C. Kinmore		4.6.15
131st Battery	Major	B. Hull		3.4.15
	Lieut	13.6. Peaton		30.6.15
	2/Lieut	9.B. Lomes		29.7.15
	2/Lieut	J.B. McKay		
19th B. AC Columns	Capt.	N. Y. Lambert		10.12.14
	2/Lieut	L. Wilfred		29.3.15
	2/Lieut	? Lockwood		28.6.15
	2/Lieut	? George		17.5.15

147

19. B⁰ᵐ R.F.A.

WAR DIARY 19ᵗʰ B - R.F.A.
or
INTELLIGENCE SUMMARY.
(Erase heading not required.)

Army Form C. 2118.

Hour, Date, Place	Summary of Events and Information	Remarks and references to Appendices
Sep 17ᵗʰ	The Brigade withdrew to Billets near OUTERSTEENE.	
" 19 - 20		
21	Now station to AMIENS.	
23	95 - 96 - 1 Section 39ᵗʰ Batty came into action at STEENBECQUE - entrained & detrained at LONGUEAU - The remaining section of 39ᵗʰ came into action with 98ᵗʰ Batty. The ready slew batty a 6 gun batty.	
26	Brigade H.Q. establish in grove dug out at CHUIGNES. Bde H.Q. moved into CHUIGNOLLES, to the river 82·³¹ₒ₂³ Bde.	
26 + 27.	The weather from 22ⁿᵈ to end of month the weather was very wet as Batteries were living in & shelters in the woods they were all thoroughly uncomfortable + wet.	
	151 Relieve 148ᵗʰ Battery:	

TRANSLATIONS.

Auberge, Aub^{ge}	Inn.
Bac	Ferry.
Cabaret, Cab^t	Inn.
Carrière	Quarry.
Cheminée	Factory Chimney.
Déversoir	Weir.
Écluse	Lock.
Étang, E^{g}	Pond.
Fontaine, Font	Spring.
Gué	Ford.
Marais	Marsh.
Moulin, M^{in}	Mill.
Nacelle	Ferry.
Puits	Well, Shaft.
Source	Spring.

121/7381

27th Division

19th Bde: R.t.A.
Vol IX
Oct 15

WAR DIARY 19th Bde R.F.A.
or
INTELLIGENCE SUMMARY.

Army Form C. 2118.

(Erase heading not required.)

Hour, Date, Place	Summary of Events and Information		Remarks and references to Appendices
	NAME	RANK	
Oct. 1.1915. 19th Bde HQrs	G.A. Smyth	Lt.Col.	Joined Brigade
	G. Temple	Capt	20.9.09
	G. Hemingworth	2/Lieut	2.11.15
	Holyhead	Lieut	17.11.15
	Alabaster	Lieut	2.7.15
	R.A.M.C		24.7.15
39th Battery R.F.A	M. FitzG. Eady	Major	10.2.15	change in list
	Rickey	Capt	3.7.15 26th Ridley to 95th
	Erid	Lieut	10.12.14 posted to 95th Bty
	Bone	2/Lt	15.5.15 / 2nd Div. on 6th
			15.5.15 / orders from 1st
			9th Div. ord attached
			12.9.15
95th Battery R.F.A	Major Richmond	Major	29.5.15
	Hubert	Capt	5.5.15
	Eaton	Lieut	1.8.15
		2/Lt	29.7.15
96th Battery R.F.A	G.E. Hindle	Major	14.5.15
	R.K.Simpson	Lieut	19.9.15
	C.E. Linne	2/Lieut	25.7.15
	E.A.H. Whitcombe	2/Lieut	4.6.15
	N. Sutherton McKinnon	2/Lieut	15
131st Battery R.F.A	B.R. Hill	Major	3.4.15
	B.B. Leader	2/Lieut	26.5.15
	H. Lewis	2/Lt	20.6.15
	J.M.McKay	2/Lt	29.7.15
19th Bde A.Column	N. Plowden	Capt.	10.12.15
	F. Willock	2/Lt	2.3.15
	J. Lockwood	2/Lt	8.6.15
	H.B. Yonge	2/Lt	17.5.15

Army Form C. 2118.

WAR DIARY
or
INTELLIGENCE SUMMARY. HQ 43rd RFA

(Erase heading not required.)

Instructions regarding War Diaries and Intelligence Summaries are contained in F.S. Regs., Part II. and the Staff Manual respectively. Title pages will be prepared in manuscript.

Hour, Date, Place	Summary of Events and Information	Remarks and references to Appendices
HQ 43rd RFA 1st Oct. 5th Oct.	The Brigade withdrew from action and went to rest at Corbie	
22	Brigade marched by GUEZNCOURT	
23	Brigade marched to BOVES THENNES	
24		
25		

M. Hoffman
Col. 43rd RFA

14/11/16

19th Bde R.F.A.

2/nov
1/nov X

121/7929

27/4/15

Nov' 15.   27 [?]
                                            Army Form C-2118.

WAR DIARY
or
INTELLIGENCE SUMMARY.
(Erase heading not required.)

19th Bde R.F.A.

Hour, Date, Place	Rank	Summary of Events and Information	Joined Bde	Remarks and references to Appendices
19th Bde H.Qrs	Lt.Col.	C.H. Smyth	23.7.14	
	Lt.	Brig. Beit Adjt 1.11.15	10.12.12	
	"	J.E. Harworth	14.11.	
	"	J.N. Alabaster R.A.M.C	28.7.	
39th Bty R.F.A	Capt	C.C. Pearson	16.5.15	
	"	C.C. Lyons	9.7.15	
	"	C.C. Bowe	15.5.15	
	2/Lt	C.J. Kerry		
95th Bty R.F.A	Major	L.H.D. Graper	27.5.15	Capt. C.G. Risley 12th Lancers transferred to 18th Division
	Lt	N.G.H. Hubert	1.8.15	
	2/Lt	G.R. Colen	29.7.15	
	"	B.C. Palmer	5.11.15	
96th Bty R.F.A	Major	H.C. Meade	14.5.15	
	Lt.	R. Kerr Simpson	28.8.15	
	2/Lt	G.A.N. Whitmile	25.4.15	
	"	L.N. Tulloch McKinnon	4.6.15	
131st Bty R.F.A.	Major	C. Bell	3.4.15	Capt. G. Temple R.F. transferred to 12th Division
	2/Lt	G. McKay	29.7.15	
	"	B.C.R. Keith	28.5.15	
	"	J.R. Henley	4.11.15	
19th Brigade A.Colm	Capt.	C.H.J. Glanstey	10.12.12	Admitted to Hospital 27.11.15
	2/Lt	C.H. Nunted	7.6.15	
	"	C.H. Neville	4.11.15	
	A.C.H.G	Lehuedes	4.11.15	
	Capt	W.D. Holford A.V.C	2.7.15	

Army Form C. 2118.

WAR DIARY
or
INTELLIGENCE SUMMARY.

19/73 of an NH

(Erase heading not required.)

Instructions regarding War Diaries and Intelligence Summaries are contained in F. S. Regs., Part II. and the Staff Manual respectively. Title pages will be prepared in manuscript.

Hour, Date, Place	Summary of Events and Information	Remarks and references to Appendices
13—11—15	Capt J.A. Smith RAMC Jour Barguedi	[signature]

6th Bde R.F.A.
Dec
vol XII

WAR DIARY or INTELLIGENCE SUMMARY

Army Form C. 2118.

December 1, 1915   19th Bde RFA

(Erase heading not required.)

Instructions regarding War Diaries and Intelligence Summaries are contained in F.S. Regs., Part II. and the Staff Manual respectively. Title pages will be prepared in manuscript.

Hour, Date, Place	Summary of Events and Information		Remarks and references to Appendices
	NAME	RANK	
19th Bde R.F.A H.Qrs	C.A. Smyth	Lt. Col.	Joined Bde 30.9.09
	J.A.C. Crick Adjt	Lt.	10.12.14
	J.B. Heyworth	Lt.	17.11.15
	G.A. Smith RAMC	Capt.	13.11.15
39th Bty R.F.A	H. Pyston	Capt.	15.5.15
	C.W. Lynne	Lt.	9.7.15
	C.R. Bone	2/Lt.	15.3.15
	S.S. Lowry	2/Lt.	4.11.15 — Admitted to Hospital 15.12.15 (Scarlet fever)
96th Bty R.F.A	L.A.D. Maker	Major	29.5.15
	F.J.H. Hulbert	Lt.	1.8.14
	W.J. Eaton	2/Lt.	29.7.15
	P.C. Palmer	2/Lt.	5.11.15
20th Bty R.F.A	G.C. Newte	Major	14.5.15
	R.K.M. Simpson	Lt.	28.8.15
	E.A.N. Whitcombe	2/Lt.	25.7.15
	L.N. Fullerton McKinnon	2/Lt.	4.6.15
131st Bty R.F.A	C.C. Hill	Major	3.4.15
	B.C. Tesler	Lt.	28.5.15
	Frewen	2/Lt.	4.11.15
	A.E.J. Selwood	2/Lt.	4.11.15
19th Bde A.C.	N.J.P. Plomley	2/Lt.	10.12.14
	B.R. McKay	2/Lt.	29.7.15
	Lowthy	2/Lt.	4.11.15
19th Bde S.A.A. Section	F.L. Lockwood	2/Lt.	7.6.15
	R. Cocks	2/Lt.	7.11.15 → Admitted to Hospital 26.12.15
	Davis A.V.C.		3.12.15

Army Form C. 2118.

WAR DIARY
or
INTELLIGENCE SUMMARY.
(Erase heading not required.)

19th Bn. R.Ir.

Hour, Date, Place	Summary of Events and Information	Remarks and references to Appendices
Dec 3.	Brigade entrained at LONGNEAU (Amiens) for Marseilles	
" 5.	Brigade arrived MARSEILLES & went into a very dirty camp at BORELY.	
" 16.	95th Battn. Lieut Hubert 2 guns 16 gunners + 100 rounds ammn. for gun embarked on S.S. Anglo Egyptian — The guns were mounted on the forecastle as a protection against Submarines.	Ammn. was loaded as the two decks uncovered
	Lieut Simpson 2 guns 16 gunners 96th Battn. were embarked on S.S. MERVILLE + the guns were mounted on the forecastle for protection against Submarines.	
	24th Nov? (?) The Brigade had its usual route march next on each of the long coasts on the lines as about thirteen men were installed — Some of the few 2nd Battn, of whom this had any experience. The 96th Battn. Irish-Dublin + Tasmania men — the boy strong bulls together them	

27th Division

95th Battery R.F.A.

$\frac{121}{4210}$

Vol I. 15.10.14 — 31.1.15

149

Army Form C. 2118.

WAR DIARY
or
INTELLIGENCE SUMMARY

(Erase heading not required.)

Instructions regarding War Diaries and Intelligence Summaries are contained in F. S. Regs., Part II. and the Staff Manual respectively. Title pages will be prepared in manuscript.

Hour, Date, Place	Summary of Events and Information	Remarks and references to Appendices
Oct 15th 1914. India	Sailed from Bombay for England on H.T. Avon.	
Nov 19th 1914.	Reached Winchester and went out under canvas. Battery split up into two four gun batteries, the 95th Commanded by Major F.B.D. Broadwith and the 131st Commanded by Captain J.C.M. Hanley, and started to mobilize.	
Dec 19th 1914	Left Winchester and marched to Portsmouth, and embarked on S.S. City of Chester for HAVRE. Disembarked and went by train to SECHER.	
Jan 7th 1915.	Thence marched to RENESCURE. Billeted at RENESCURE until Jan 17th and then marched to HERSKEN and from went into billets.	
Jan 17th 1915. 7.30 AM	Took over guns of 67th Battery in position in firing line. Remained in action in the position until 5.30 pm Jan 29th firing a few rounds daily at the enemy support trenches. Blen took over the guns of the Battery, which had been brought up, by 67th Battery.	
Jan 29th 1915.	New position a bend of DICKEBUSCH pond. Original position but once shelled by the enemy.	
Jan 31st	Still in position a bend of DICKEBUSCH POND. Slight burst and shows of F/B Shrapnel. Nothing to report.	

Leon dg 95th Battery R.F.A.
Major R.F.A.

121/4556

27th Division
95th Bttry (15th Bde) R.F.A.
Vol II. 1 – 27.2.15

Nil

Army Form C. 2118.

WAR DIARY
or
INTELLIGENCE SUMMARY
(Erase heading not required.)

Instructions regarding War Diaries and Intelligence Summaries are contained in F. S. Regs., Part II. and the Staff Manual respectively. Title pages will be prepared in manuscript.

Hour, Date, Place	Summary of Events and Information	Remarks and references to Appendices
Feb 1st 1915 DICKEBUSCH.	Still in action back of pond.	
2ᵃᵐ	do	
3	do	
4	do	
5	do	
6	do — Nothing unusual to record.	
6⁵⁰ 7ᵃ 8 9⁵⁰ 10 11⁴⁰ 12 13ᵖᵐ		
14⁵ 15	Enemy commenced attack about 4 pm — not heavy artillery fire. Battery opened fire about 4 pm and continued in action until about 7 am. Next morning firing at varying intervals almost without stopping all the time. Relief. Artillery fire reported on most severely by infantry.	
16ᵗʰ	An alarm at 9.45 pm — fire ceased at his 7 rounds.	
17ᵗʰ 18 19 20 21 22 23 24⁵	Nothing unusual occurred. Only ordinary entrenching carried out.	
25 26 27⁵	Battery shaking. Weather throughout to week generally bad — much rain. Some snow — the ground towards end of month wet into fog.	

J.C. Brolyn/ Lieut Major RHA
Commanding Battery

24th Division

95th Batty: R.F.A.

Vol III. 1 – 31.3.15

Army Form C. 2118.

WAR DIARY
or
INTELLIGENCE SUMMARY
(Erase heading not required.)

Hour, Date, Place	Summary of Events and Information	Remarks and references to Appendices
March 1st 1915. PICKLEBUSCH	Still in action on South of road.	
2" 12-45 AM	Opened fire to support infantry on German trench. Remained	
" 2"	in action until 3 AM. 3/3/15.	
" 3" 4" + 5"	Nothing to record	
" 6"	Heavy bombardment of enemy's trenches. Fired at intervals on	
	enemy trenches + support trenches from 6-30 AM till 8 P.M.	
" 7" + 8"	Routine firing	
" 9"	Bombarded enemy support trenches 6 pm till 4-30 pm.	
" 10"	Routine firing	
" 11"	Fired on Support trenches at intervals throughout the day.	
" 12"	Support trenches. 3-15 P.M. Hotandochin Farm, pill Q1, Batteries.	
" 13"	Fired on support trenches	
" 14"	Fired a few rounds during the morning. At 5-30 seen enemy building	
	commenced heavy fire, and exploded mines under tunnel	
	and some trenches, making infantry attack at same time.	
" 15"	Opened fire at once. fire kept up at rapid rate until 7 P.M.	
	Commenced firing at round at ½ reason, and kept on till 11.15	
	until 7-15 P.M.	
	3-15 P.M. S.O.S. Signal received. Fired from trench and then stopped by	
" 16"	signal sent in	

Army Form C. 2118.

WAR DIARY
or
INTELLIGENCE SUMMARY

(Erase heading not required.)

Instructions regarding War Diaries and Intelligence Summaries are contained in F. S. Regs., Part II. and the Staff Manual respectively. Title pages will be prepared in manuscript.

Hour, Date, Place	Summary of Events and Information	Remarks and references to Appendices
17ᵗʰ 18ᵗʰ 19ᵗʰ 20ᵗʰ 21ˢᵗ 22ⁿᵈ 23ʳᵈ 24ᵗʰ 25ᵗʰ 26ᵗʰ 27ᵗʰ 28ᵗʰ 29ᵗʰ 30ᵗʰ & 31	Nothing killed. Enemy very quiet.	

27th Division

131st Batty R+A.

121/4210

Vol I. 27.11.14 — 31.1.15

Army Form C. 2118.

WAR DIARY
or
INTELLIGENCE SUMMARY.
(Erase heading not required.)

Hour, Date, Place	Summary of Events and Information	Remarks and references to Appendices
27th November 1914. Winchester	Battery was formed from 95th Battery R.F.A. in camp. Capt E.C. Manly R.F.A. and half personnel & equipment of 95th Battery R.F.A. forming a nucleus which was reinforced by the addition of an extra gun + personnel & equipment. Remainder (½) left Officers:- Capt J. Cullwaring R.F.A. Lt H. Fielden 2 Lt. H. Hinwood + 2 Lt. C. B. Trinne	
19th December	Marched Winchester - Southampton + embarked S.S. "Norian" + disembarked at Havre 20th/21st	
21st December. HAVRE	Entrained + proceeded to ARQUES + marched from there to RENESCURE to billets	
7th January RENESCURE	Marched RENESCURE - PRADELLES	
8th January PRADELLES	" PRADELLES - HEKSKEN	
17th January HEKSKEN	" HEKSKEN - DICKEBUSCH, and engaged enemy trenches SOUTH of ST ELOI 18.1.15. Lieut A Fielden posted to 19th Bde Amm Coln. Lt. B. Dolvé posted from 19th Bde Amm Coln.	

157

Army Form C. 2118.

WAR DIARY
or
INTELLIGENCE SUMMARY.
(Erase heading not required.)

Instructions regarding War Diaries and Intelligence Summaries are contained in F.S. Regs., Part II. and the Staff Manual respectively. Title pages will be prepared in manuscript.

Hour, Date, Place	Summary of Events and Information	Remarks and references to Appendices
17.1.15 DICKEBUSCH (H.35.a.5.0.)	Nothing to report. Ordered not to fire unless enemies artillery shelled our infantry trenches.	(Reference Map. 1/40.000. Sheet 28. N.W.)
18.1.15 " "	Ditto	
19.1.15 " "	Received orders to move to new position on the bank of L'ETANG de DICKEBUSCH. Prepared a road through the mud and removed one wagon. Misty. New position reconnoitred for occupation at H. Sec. 28. d. 3.1. on bank.	
20.1.15 " "	Continued repair of road and removed 2nd wagon. Mud very deep.	
21.1.15 " "		
2.5 p.m. 22.1.15 " "	Fired 20 rounds at enemy's battery reported by aeroplane in S.E. corner 0.9. Range 2600 yds on 14.B.A.13.S.3. 15' Elevation.	
23.1.15 " "	Continued preparation for moving. Very misty. Got out two remaining wagons.	
24.1.15 " "	Bng new pits on new position ready for occupation. Pits occupied by 67th Bty RFA who took over 131st Bty's Zone of fire + targets. Bng new pits for occupation. Weather foggy.	
25.1.15 " "		
26.1.15 " (H.28.2.3.1)	Occupied new position and opened it occupied under cover of fog. Received orders to be prepared to fire at following Bty Zones at 014.a.7.7.; 09.2, SEcorner, 015.a.9.3. locality. Bg. Zones reported at 015.a.3.2.; 08d9.7. Night Zone 08.a.SW.4.58.	

Ayer Gates Forms/C. 2118/10.

Army Form C. 2118.

WAR DIARY
or
INTELLIGENCE SUMMARY.
(Erase heading not required.)

Instructions regarding War Diaries and Intelligence Summaries are contained in F.S. Regs., Part II and the Staff Manual respectively. Title pages will be prepared in manuscript.

Hour, Date, Place	Summary of Events and Information	Remarks and references to Appendices
DICKEBUSCH (H28d3.) 26.1.15 (continued)	Ready to open fire at 2.30 p.m. Very misty	(Ref ¹/₄₀,₀₀₀ Sheet 28. N.W.)
27.1.15	Improved position. Did not fire	
28.1.15	" " " "	
4.25 p.m 29.1.15	Fired 10 (ten) rounds at Enemy's battery located at O9, range 5800 a. s/b 15' E.	
10.0 a.m 30.1.15	Opened fire on Enemy Battery at O8a. 4b. 94. Range 1100	8 Rounds Shrapnel
12 noon	" " " " 98 2810 " " 4500	8 " "
2.3 p.m	" " " " O8a. 9b. 80 " " 4460	8 " "
9.40 a.m 31.1.15	Endeavoured to register mark O7. Weather conditions made observation impossible owing to snowstorm. Fire 13 rounds Rg 4000 Cor 150	
12 noon 31.1.15		

J. Mulvaney
Captain R.A.
F.C. 131 B[de] R.F.A.

121/4636

27th Division

131st Battery (19th Bde) R.F.A.

Vol II   31.1. — 27.2.15

160

Army Form C. 2118.

WAR DIARY
or
INTELLIGENCE SUMMARY.
(Erase heading not required.)

Instructions regarding War Diaries and Intelligence Summaries are contained in F.S. Regs., Part II. and the Staff Manual respectively. Title pages will be prepared in manuscript.

Hour, Date, Place	Summary of Events and Information	Remarks and references to Appendices
2.30 p.m. 31·1·15. DICKEBUSCH (H 28 a 3.1)	Obtained registration of wood O77. 370 cor 154 a 6/S 0'E fired 12 Rounds	Ref Map 20.000. Sheet 28.
10.15 a.m. 2·2·15 "	Zone St ELOI. enemies Trenches fired on to silence infantry fire. fired 11 Rounds 40-43 cor 154 a 6/S 10' to 0'E	
2·2·15 "	" " " did not fire	
3·2·15 "	" " "	
9·45 a.m. 4·2·15 "	Zone St ELOI 40-43 cor 154 a 6/S 10' to 0'E Zone registered 17 Rounds fired	
12.5 p.m. 4·2·15 "	Ordered to assist infantry in Zone St ELOI fired 29 Rounds " to fire 6 Rds Treby C at Battery O 82.6.1. Rg 5050. cor	
2.35 p.m. 5·2·15 "	" " 154 30'15 A 6/S.	
10.38 a.m. 6·2·15 "	Zone from farm O 8 o 2.8. to N.E. corner Wood O77 registered by line 18 Rds shrapnel.	
2.0 p.m. 7·2·15 "	Obtained line range for Battery Zone. 20 Rounds	
7.0 a.m. 8·2·15 "	Ordered to fire 12 Rounds Shrapnel at farm O 8 o 2 8.	
4.45 p.m. 8·2·15 "	" " 8 " " "	
6.45 a.m. 9·2·15 "	" " 4 " " " in strong N Wind thawing	
8.55 a.m. 9·2·15 "	Re-Registered line to Zone + corrected 7 Rounds fired	
10·2·15 "	Nothing to report	
11·2·15 "	" " "	
12·2·15 "	" " "	
13·2·15 "	" " "	

(73989) W4141—463. 400,000. 9/14. H.&J.Ltd. Forms/C. 2118/10.

161

Army Form C. 2118.

WAR DIARY
or
INTELLIGENCE SUMMARY.
(Erase heading not required.)

Instructions regarding War Diaries and Intelligence Summaries are contained in F.S. Regs., Part II. and the Staff Manual respectively. Title pages will be prepared in manuscript.

Hour, Date, Place	Summary of Events and Information	Remarks and references to Appendices
4.2 p.m. 14.2.15 Souupas?	Engaged enemies infantry entrenched between St Eloi in co-operation with counter-attack by infantry. Two guns of battery having been deployed to PoPERINGHE for overhaul. Enemy guns in action. Cease Fire at 7.0 a.m. 15.2.15. Rounds fired 669 by two guns. No casualties	Artillery thanks by G.O.C. 5th Corps.
9.40 p.m. 15.2.15 "	Ordered to assist infantry at St Eloi. Fired 12 rounds ordered to stop	
10.15 p.m. 16.2.15 "	Ordered to assist infantry at St Eloi. Fired 8 rounds	
17.2.15 "	Did not fire	
4.0 p.m. 18.2.15 "	Fired at house O 8 d 4.1. Observed to hit.	
10.50 a.m. 19.2.15 "	" at wood O 8. Fired 7 rounds of Shrapnel.	
12.18 p.m. 20.2.15 "	Routine shooting at 2 batteries located in Zone 4 rounds each	
1.46 p.m. 21.2.15 "	" " " " " " " "	
11.45 a.m. 22.2.15 "	" " " " " " " "	
11.26 a.m. 23.2.15 "	Fired 8 Shrapnel at Sap head at corner of O.7 N.E. Observed to knock Sap shield out of parallel	
12.40 p.m. "	Fired 6 Shrapnel to Trench artarm O 8 a 2.8.	
3.6 p.m. "	Fired at 2 batteries located in Zone 4 rounds at each	
24.2.15 "	Did not fire	
25.2.15 "	" " "	
26.2.15 "	" " "	
27.2.15 "	" " "	

Antony Ley Capt R.F.A
O.C. 131 B.R.F.A.

121/4779

27th Division

131st Battery (19th Brigade) R.F.A.

Vol III. 26.2 — 29.3.15

Army Form C. 2118.

WAR DIARY
or
INTELLIGENCE SUMMARY.
(Erase heading not required.)

Instructions regarding War Diaries and Intelligence Summaries are contained in F.S. Regs., Part II and the Staff Manual respectively. Title pages will be prepared in manuscript.

Hour, Date, Place	Summary of Events and Information	Remarks and references to Appendices
28.2.15 to 1.3.15.	Fit. of fire.	
12.55 a.m. 2. 3.15 Same posn.	Opened fire on enemy's support trenches SOUTH of S.E.101. Action finished at about 2.30 a.m. 139 Rounds fired.	
12.35 p.m. " "	Fired 10 rounds of Percussion Shrapnel at Enemy's Sap head at N.E. corner of Wood O.9. Seventh round put Sap head & stairs damaged Sap and enemy's trench at edge of wood. Routine firing. Nothing to report. 20 Rounds.	
4.26 p.m. 3.3.15 " "	" " " " " "	
4.15 p.m. 4.3.15 " "	Did not fire.	
5.3.15 " "	Registered new zone from PICCADILLY FARM. to 3°. North. 10 Rds.	
8.30 a.m. 6.3.15 " "	Routine firing. Support trenches 321 Rounds.	
4.15 p.m. 6.3.15 " "	Did not fire. Nothing to report.	
7.3.15. " "	" " Nothing to report.	
8.3.15. " "	Did not fire.	
6.0 p.m. 9.3.15 " "	Fired on enemy's support trenches during attack by infantry on enemy's trenches. Rounds 87.	
10.3.15 " "	Did not fire.	
10.35 a.m. 11.3.15 " "	Fired on enemy's support trenches. 21 Rounds.	
11.45 a.m. " "	" " " " 10 Rounds.	
1.50 p.m. " "	" " " " 10 Rounds.	
2.45 p.m. " "	" " " " 32 "	
3.45 p.m. " "	" " " " 12 "	
3.10 p.m. " "	Registered HOLLANDSCHESCHOR FARM. 27 "	
5.0 " "	Piccadilly Farm. m/star shell 5 Rounds	
4.0 a.m. 12. 3.15 " "	Fired 3 Star Shell. On tails to burst, one burst, shroff. high. Rounds asst is too slight for present star shell.	

Army Form C. 2118.

WAR DIARY
or
INTELLIGENCE SUMMARY.
(Erase heading not required.)

Instructions regarding War Diaries and Intelligence Summaries are contained in F.S. Regs., Part II and the Staff Manual respectively. Title pages will be prepared in manuscript.

Hour, Date, Place	Summary of Events and Information	Remarks and references to Appendices
2.26 p.m. 13.3.15 St. Eloi trench	Fired on enemies support trenches in Zone. 25 Rounds	
3.15 a.m. 14.3.15 "	Routine firing at Artillery Targets in Zone. 15 Shrapnel	
5.30 p.m. 14.3.15 " (1)	To repel enemies attack on zone during attack on St. Eloi. Action continued all night of 14/15. 825 Rounds fired.	
15.3.15 "	Enemies in observation ready to open fire.	
16.3.15 "	Did not fire. Nothing to report.	
17.3.15 "	" " " "	
18.3.15 "	" " " "	
19.3.15 "	" " " "	
20.3.15 "	Registered target O.9.a.0.0 with Aeroplane observer.	
21.3.15 "	" S.O.9.2.1.4 and O.8.7.2.1. " "	
22.3.15 "	" O.8.2.8.6 " O.8.a.9.5 " "	
3.45 p.m. 21.3.15 "	Saphead in front of our No.14 trench. 3 hits observed.	
10.0 a.m. 23.3.15 "	Battery at O.8.a.8.5.8. Routine firing.	
24-29.3.15 "	Did not fire. Nothing to report.	

Mulcahy Capt RFA
Lt. 131 By RFA

24.3.15.

29th Division

131st Batty: R.F.A.

Vol IV 31.3 — 27.4.15

Army Form C. 2118

WAR DIARY
or
INTELLIGENCE SUMMARY.
(Erase heading not required.)

Instructions regarding War Diaries and Intelligence Summaries are contained in F.S. Regs., Part II and the Staff Manual respectively. Title pages will be prepared in manuscript.

Place	Hour, Date	Summary of Events and Information	Remarks and references to Appendices
WESTHOEK	9.4.15.	Distant fire MG. Registered gun.	
"	10.4.15.	Registered target on gun.	
"	11.4.15.	Registered enemy fire trenches. Range 2630.	
"	12.4.15.	" support " " 2800.	
"	13.4.15.	" Snipes Copse " 2800.	
"	14.4.15.	Shelled support trenches.	
"	15.4.15.	Registered front on gun.	
"	16.4.15.	Registered points with aeroplane observation in J 15.	
"	17.4.15.	Did not fire.	
"	18.4.15.	Registered another target on gun.	
"	19.4.15.	10 rounds at enemy observation station, effective.	
"	20.4.15.	Shelled enemy supports in RENTELBEEK valley.	
"	21.4.15.	Engaged enemy guns.	
"	22.4.15.	2nd Lt. J. T. RICHARDS attached L Battery for instruction purposes.	

168

Army Form C. 2118.

WAR DIARY
or
INTELLIGENCE SUMMARY.
(Erase heading not required.)

Instructions regarding War Diaries and Intelligence Summaries are contained in F.S. Regs., Part II and the Staff Manual respectively. Title pages will be prepared in manuscript.

Hour, Date, Place	Summary of Events and Information	Remarks and references to App[endices]
WESTHOEK 23.4.15.	Battery switched 130° E. support Canadians.	
" 24.4.15.	Fired all day in support of Canadians, who were replaced during the day by Dorset Troops.	
" 25.4.15.	Largest targets all day in support of 28th Division, to the North.	
" 26.4.15.	Supporting 28th Division to the North East; observation station at point 37 (D 20 A.4.9.) Range 4000"	
" 27.4.15.	As on 26.4.15. {Wounded 2 other ranks — Gunning 1 — {Killed 1 horse Wounded 5 —	
" 28.4.15.	" " {Wounded 1 other ranks — {Killed, 2 horses — Wounded 9 — Gunning 3.	
" 29.4.15.	" " {Killed — 3 other ranks — Wounded 6 — {Killed — 6 horses Gunning —	
	Battery & wagon lines are now shelled from N.W. & S.E.	

P.W.W[...]
Major R.F.A.
Commanding 131st Battery R.F.A.
30.4.15.
12 noon.

(73989) W4141—463. 400,000. 9/14. H.&J.Ltd. Forms/C. 2118/10.

www.ingramcontent.com/pod-product-compliance
Lightning Source LLC
Chambersburg PA
CBHW081555160426
43191CB00011B/1942